Coloring mandala coloring books can be a relaxing and meditative activity. Here are some tips for coloring mandala coloring books:

Choose your color palette: Decide on a color palette before starting. You can choose a complementary color scheme or use analogous colors. You can also use colors that represent a particular mood or emotion.

Start from the center: Start coloring from the center of the mandala and work your way outwards. This will help you create a balanced and harmonious design.

Use different shades: Use different shades of the same color to create depth and dimension in your mandala. This can also help you create a gradient effect.

Use white space: Don't feel like you have to color every single space in the mandala. Leaving some white space can create a beautiful contrast and give your mandala a more open and airy feeling.

Blend colors: Blend colors together to create a smoother transition between colors. You can use a blending tool or your finger to blend colors.

Experiment with different mediums: Try coloring with different mediums such as pencils, markers, or watercolors to see which one you prefer. Each medium will create a different effect.

Take your time: Don't rush through coloring your mandala. Take your time and enjoy the process. It's okay to take breaks and come back to it later.

Remember that there are no rules when it comes to coloring mandalas. The most important thing is to have fun and enjoy the process!